PIANO • VOCAL • GUITAR

NEIL DIAMOND

UP ON THE ROOF

SONGS FROM THE BRILL BUILDING

ISBN 0-7935-2951-4 .

Cover Photo by Eugene Adebari
Back Cover Illustration by William Dely

7777 W. BLUEMOUND RD. P.O. BOX 13819 MILWAUKEE, WI 53213

C O N T E N T S

In 1958, I booked a professional recording studio and recorded demonstration tapes of five songs I had written. I'd been writing for eighteen months, and it was time to test the waters to see if I had any real talent. Eight years later *Solitary Man* was released, and I was a hit recording artist. Between those two mileposts was a magical time for me, as I slowly but inevitably drifted from the academic world of New York University into the music world—specifically Tin Pan Alley, about six square blocks of Manhattan filled with music publishing companies, record companies, managers, agents, recording studios and swarms of other songwriters, people just like me with whom I could share the agony and also the sheer fun of the music business.

If you were signed by a music publisher as a staff writer, you got a regular weekly check. Otherwise, you lived from week to week on the advances paid by publishers for the copyrights to your songs. If the publisher liked a song, you got to make a demo, and you also probably got an advance on future royalties, which was usually enough to get you through the week.

Almost all the songs on this album were written during the years when I was knocking on those doors in Tin Pan Alley. I remember these songs, but I remember them in a special way: I was in the waiting room while they were being written inside, often by people from my neighborhood, sometimes even my school. Therefore, anything was possible for me.

THE WRITERS AND THE SONGS

I was usually the lead vocalist on the demos of my own songs. I used the fee that would normally have gone to a "professional" demo singer and instead hired an additional musician or even some background singers. That's how I met **Ellie Greenwich.** Check out any of my 1966-68 recordings, and you'll hear Ellie and **Jeff Barry** singing the background parts. (They also, not incidentally, ended up producing all those early hit recordings.) Ellie had enormous status as a writer, but she still took on background-singing gigs—mostly for fun, maybe to hang out with the singers she'd worked with for years or maybe to keep an eye out for new talent. Whatever the reason, Ellie sang even for unknowns like me. After our demo session, she brought me over to meet her husband Jeff, all 6'6" of him, bursting with enthusiasm and talent. They had already written *Do Wah Diddy Diddy* and would later write the classic *River Deep - Mountain High*— as they had *Chapel Of Love, Be My Baby* and *Da Do Ron Ron (When He Walked Me Home)*—with Phil Spector, a west-coast writer/producer/musical innovator who was a frequent presence in Tin Pan Alley, co-writing with an assortment of New York's best songwriters.

Jeff and Ellie somehow managed to get me signed, as a staff writer and possible recording artist, to Trio Music—in the Brill Building, the heart of Tin Pan Alley. Trio was owned and run by the legendary songwriting team of **Jerry Leiber** and **Mike Stoller**, who wrote *Love Potion Number Nine* and the lyric to *I (Who Have Nothing)*. They also wrote *Hound Dog, Jailhouse Rock* and *Kansas City*, while Jerry Leiber wrote **Spanish Harlem** with Phil Spector. I spent that year among songwriting legends: Leiber and Stoller across the hall, Jeff Barry and Ellie Greenwich next door and Phil Spector passing through on the way to and from L.A. I was in songwriter's heaven, rubbing elbows with some of my idols and trying to learn all I could from them.

Just down the street at Don Kirshner's and Al Nevins' Aldon Music were writers from another peak of pop songwriting's Mount Olympus. They were the 'child prodigies', just out of their teens yet writing some of the greatest pop songs of the day. One of Aldon's staff writing teams was the even-then-legendary **Carole King** and her husband, lyricist **Gerry Goffin**. Among the dozens of wonderful songs they wrote were *Up On The Roof* and *Will You Love Me Tomorrow* as well as *The Loco-Motion, Hey Girl* and *(You Make Me Feel Like) A Natural Woman* (with Jerry Wexler). One day, while tagging along with my pals from the Tokens (hitting big at the time with *The Lion Sleeps Tonight*), I glimpsed Goffin and King at work in their office. In this tiny room with only a small couch and an old upright piano worked America's number one musical couple. Carole looked like a teenager to me, seven or eight months pregnant at the time, intense and serious beyond her years. Husband Gerry, on the other hand, seemed an island of cool brilliance. Check out his lyrics for verification.

The other top Aldon Music husband-and-wife team, **Barry Mann** and **Cynthia Weil**, wrote *You've Lost That Lovin' Feelin'* (with Phil Spector) and a whole gang of other gigantic hits, including *Uptown, (You're My) Soul And Inspiration* and *On Broadway* (with Leiber and Stoller).

Aldon Music was a really happening place. They also had the hit writer and recording artist **Neil Sedaka**. Neil had *I Go Ape* and *Oh! Carol* when he was just out of high school (my high school!). He and his co-writer, lyricist **Howard Greenfield**, wrote hits for himself (*Calendar Girl, Breaking Up Is Hard To Do*) and also for the number one female singer of the day, Connie Francis (*Where The Boys Are*). The Sedaka/Greenfield song that we chose for this album, **Happy Birthday Sweet Sixteen**, takes on new meaning at this point in my life with my two daughters past that age, so I'll dedicate it to Marjorie and Elyn... and to Dara Sedaka, too.

Another pair of pop giants of that time was the unlikely team of **Doc Pomus** and **Mort Shuman**, who also worked out of the Brill Building, as staff writers for Hill And Range Music (then a giant music publishing juggernaut). Pomus and Shuman wrote tons of great songs, including *A Teenager In Love* and *This Magic Moment*. I've chosen one of my favorites that's a bit less known, **Sweets For My Sweet**, as well as one that's a classic: **Save**

The Last Dance For Me, which everybody loves. I spent an afternoon writing with Doc Pomus and can tell you that he was a generous and talented man who treated the ideas of an unknown with a respect that made me feel honored and accepted. Mort Shuman later moved to Paris, where he achieved added acclaim and stardom as a singer-songwriter.

Hill And Range Music also had an inside track to the greatest musical phenomenon of the time—**Elvis Presley**. Their gifted writer **Otis Blackwell** wrote some of Elvis' best-known early hits, including *Don't Be Cruel*, *All Shook Up* and *Return To Sende*r as well as *Great Balls Of Fire*, *So Fine* and *Fever* (as John Davenport) with various co-writers.

Also working out of the Brill Building and at a peak of the song-writer's Mount Olympus was the musically and lyrically sophisti-cated team of **Burt Bacharach** and **Hal David**, whose amazing body of work includes *Don't Make Me Over* and *Do You Know The Way To San Jose?* as well as the Academy Award-winner *Raindrops Keep Fallin' On My Head*, *The Look Of Love* and *Alfie*, all greats.

There were also lots of talented songwriters just coming up In those days, including **Carole Bayer Sager** and **Toni Wine**, who started their hit-writing careers with *A Groovy Kind Of Love*. Toni went on to co-write (with Irwin Levine) Tony Orlando and Dawn's gigantic record *Candida*, while Carole would later win an Oscar for her lyric to the song *Arthur's Theme (The Best That You Can Do)* and write dozens of other wonderful lyrics, including *Nobody Does It Better*, *They're Playing Our Song*—a Broadway musical—and, more recently, *That's What Friends Are For.*

By 1964, after a series of moves from one publisher to another, I had worked my advances up from fifty dollars a song to a peak of two hundred dollars (for a song called *Measles*—I guess it wasn't contagious). I wasn't doing bad, but never once in those six years did I come up with a hit—unless you count Pat Boone's

1962 recording of *Ten Lonely Guys*, which I wrote with nine colaborators late one night in the offices of the Roosevelt Music Company.

On the original demo, I sang lead along with the other nine lonely guys, my pals and fellow dreamers: **Bob Feldman, Richard Gottehrer** and **Jerry Goldstein** (*My Boyfriend's Back*), **Stanley Kahan** and **Eddie Snyder** (*A Hundred Pounds Of Clay*, with Luther Dixon; Eddie Snyder also wrote the lyric, with my buddy Charlie Singleton, for *Strangers In The Night* and *Spanish Eyes*), **Lockie Edwards, Jr.** (*Mr. Wishing Well*—which he co-wrote with the next lonely guy), **Larry Weiss** (*Rhinestone Cowboy, Bend Me, Shape Me* with Scott English), **Wes Farrell** (*Hang On Sloopy* with Bert Berns—who would soon be president of Bang Records, the label that gave me my first hits) and **Cliff Adams**. For various reasons, some of us used pseudonyms, mine being 'Mark Lewis'. I guess I must have been signed to another company at the time.

> *"On the roof's the only place I know*
> *where you just have to wish to make it so."**

I shared that same roof, and those same wishes, with so many other young songwriters of the late 1950s and early 1960s in and around Tin Pan Alley and the Brill Building. The songs on this album were a part of my life and of my highest songwriting aspirations, and I thank these writers for proving that magic could be made with words and music.

—Edited by Tom Hensley

T H A N K S

My thanks to the original artist who first made the songs on this album come alive on record for me:

The Righteous Brothers
You've Lost That Lovin' Feelin'

The Drifters
Up On The Roof

Save The Last Dance For Me

Sweets For My Sweet

The Clovers
Love Potion Number Nine

The Shirelles
Will You Love Me Tomorrow

Elvis Presley
Don't Be Cruel (To A Heart That's True)

The Exciters
Do Wah Diddy Diddy

Ben E. King
I (Who Have Nothing)

Spanish Harlem

Dionne Warwick
Don't Make Me Over

Do You Know The Way To San Jose?

Ike and Tina Turner
River Deep - Mountain High

The Mindbenders
A Groovy Kind Of Love

Neil Sedaka
Happy Birthday Sweet Sixteen

Pat Boone
Ten Lonely Guys

—Neil Diamond

YOU'VE LOST THAT LOVIN' FEELIN'

Words and Music by BARRY MANN,
CYNTHIA WEIL and PHIL SPECTOR

You nev- er close your eyes __ an - y -
wel- come look __ in your

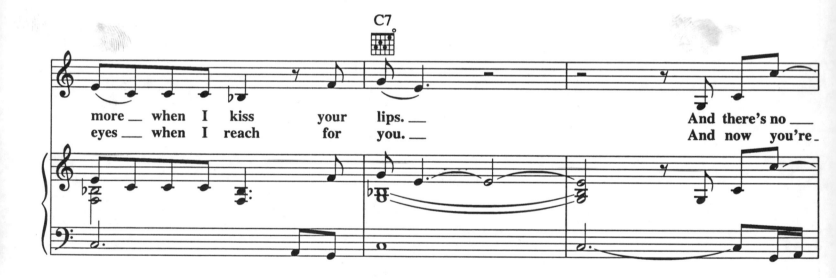

more __ when I kiss your lips. __
eyes __ when I reach for you. __

And there's no
And now you're __

__ ten- der- ness like be - fore __ in your fin ger-
__ start- ing to crit- i - cize __ lit- tle things I

C7   Dm7

tips. _____
do. _____

You're try - ing   hard   not   to   show it
It makes me   just feel   like   cry - in'

Em7   Fmaj7   Fmaj7/G   G7

ba - by,   but   ba - by, ___   ba - by   I   know   it. ___
ba - by   'cause ba - by, ___   some-thing beau - ti - ful's dy - ing. ___

C   Dm/C   G

You've lost   that   lov - in' feel - ing,   woh __ that

C   Dm7/C

lov - in' feel - ing.   You've lost that   lov - in' feel - ing. Now it's

gone,　　gone,　　gone,　　woh.

no chord

Now there's no

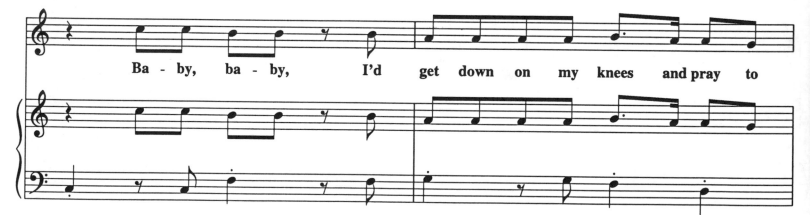

Ba - by, ba - by, I'd get down on my knees and pray to

you, if you would on - ly love

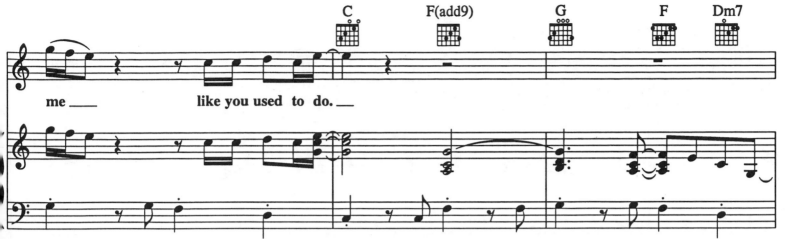

me ____ like you used to do. ____

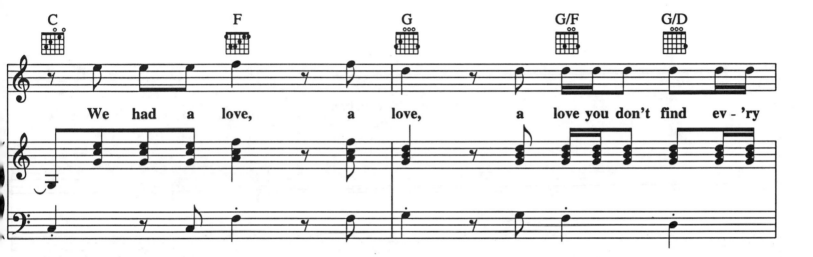

We had a love, a love, a love you don't find ev - 'ry

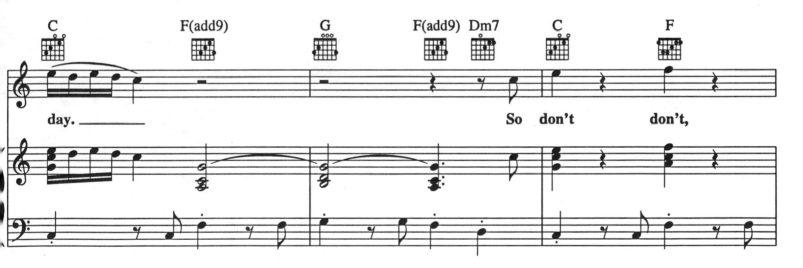

day. ____ So don't don't,

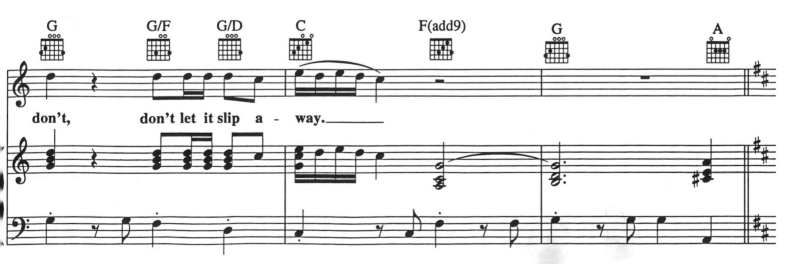

don't, don't let it slip a - way. _____

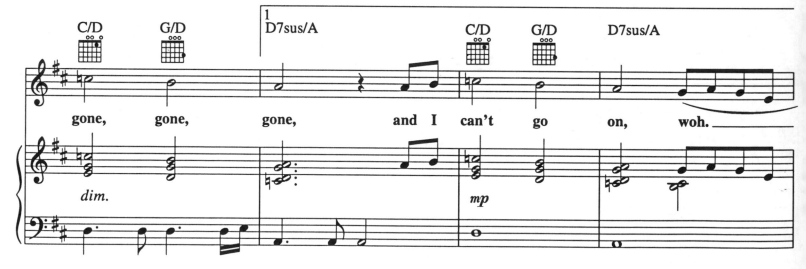

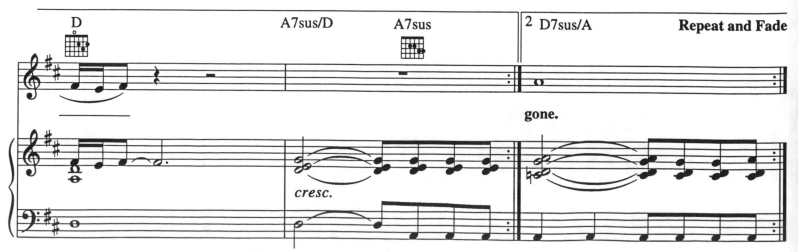

UP ON THE ROOF

Words and Music by GERRY GOFFIN
and CAROLE KING

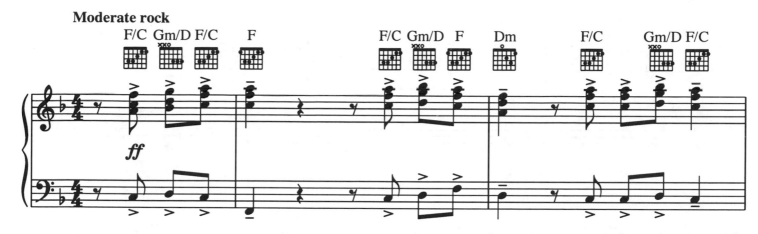

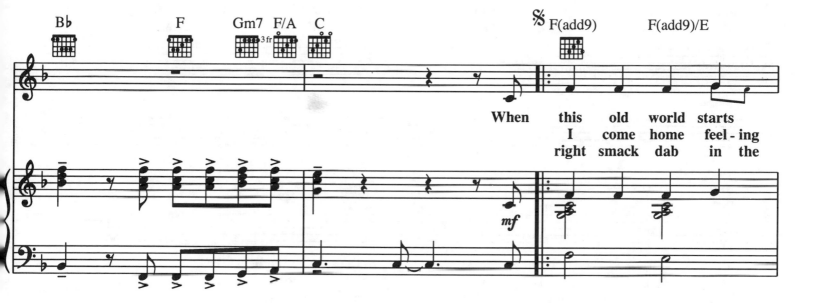

When this old world starts
I come home feel - ing
right smack dab in the

get - tin' me down and peo - ple are just too much for me to
tired __ and down beat and I'll go up where the air is fresh and
mid - dle of town I found a par - a - dise that's trou - ble

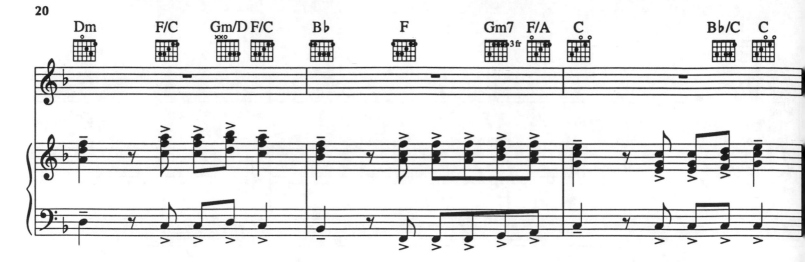

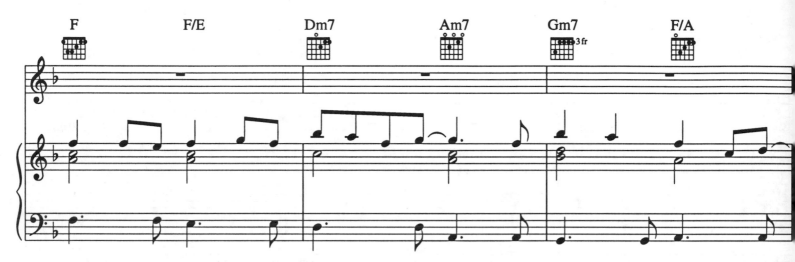

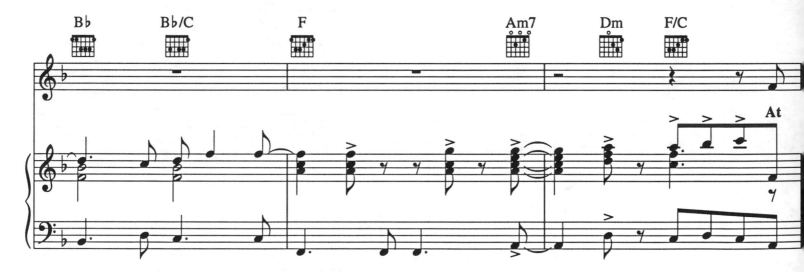

night the stars put on a show for free

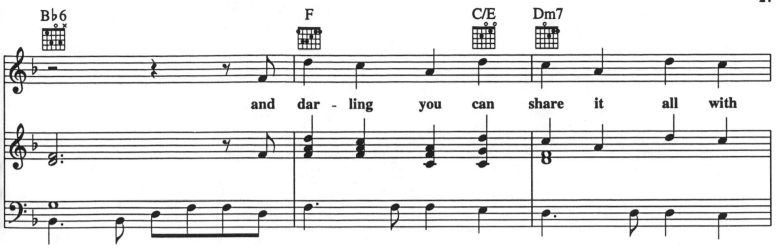

and dar - ling you can share it all with

D.S. al Coda

me. _____ I keep on tell - in' you that

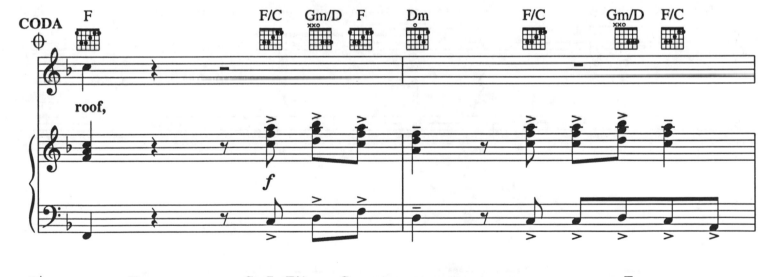

roof,

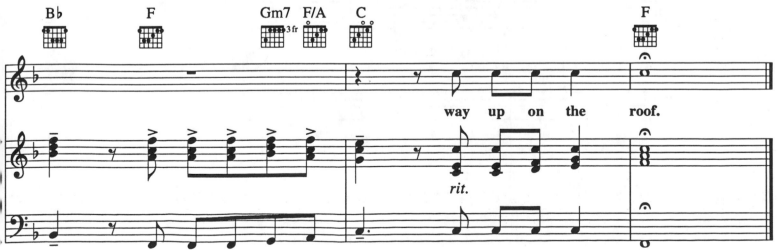

way up on the roof.

LOVE POTION NUMBER NINE

Words and Music by JERRY LEIBER
and MIKE STOLLER

DON'T BE CRUEL
(TO A HEART THAT'S TRUE)

Words and Music by OTIS BLACKWELL
and ELVIS PRESLEY

CODA

Let's

walk up to the preach - er.

Let us both say, "I do." ___

Then you'll know ___ you have me and

I know I'll have you, too. ___ Don't be cruel ___

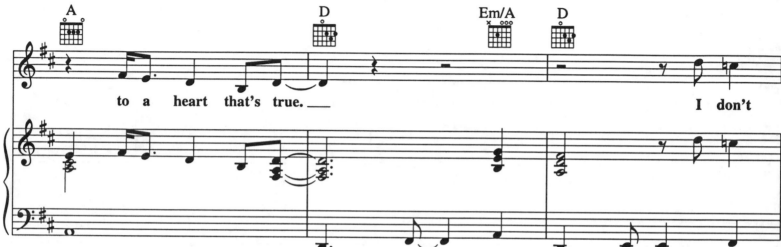

to a heart that's true. ___ I don't

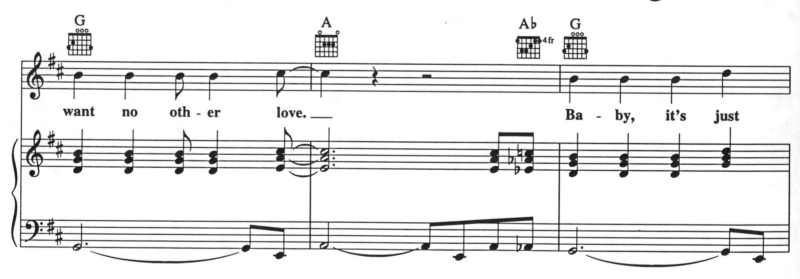

want no oth-er love. ___ Ba-by, it's just

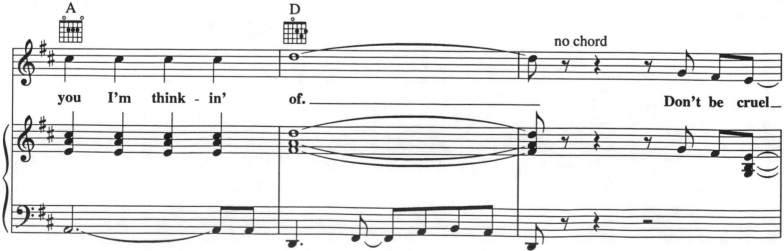

you I'm think-in' of. _____ Don't be cruel ___

WILL YOU LOVE ME TOMORROW

Words and Music by GERRY GOFFIN
and CAROLE KING

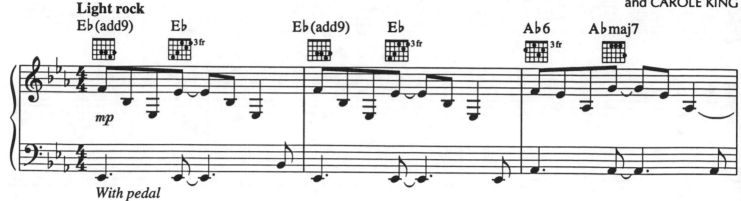

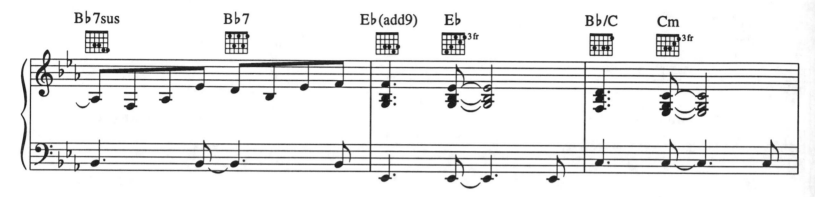

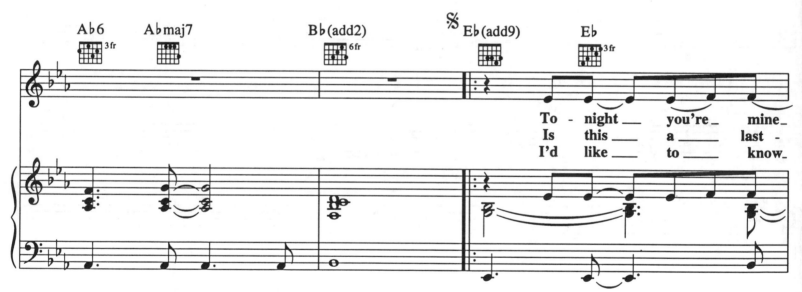

To - night ___ you're ___ mine ___
Is this ___ a ___ last -
I'd like ___ to ___ know ___

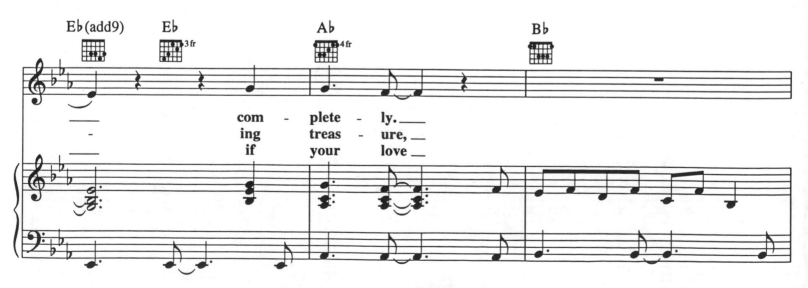

com - plete - ly. ___
ing treas - ure, ___
if your love ___

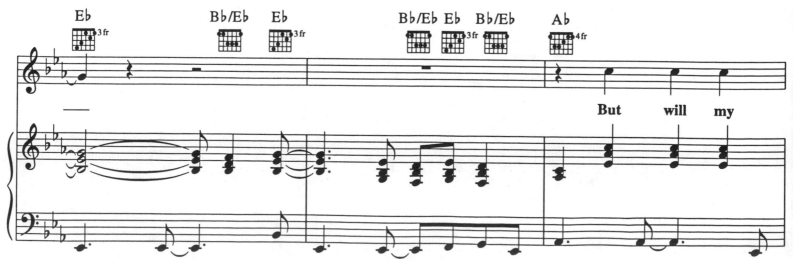

heart be bro - ken ___ when the night ___

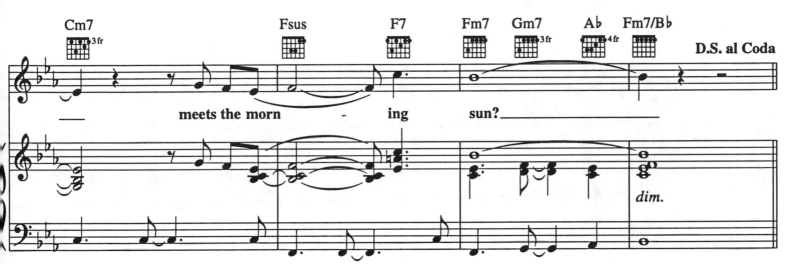

___ meets the morn - ing sun? _____

D.S. al Coda

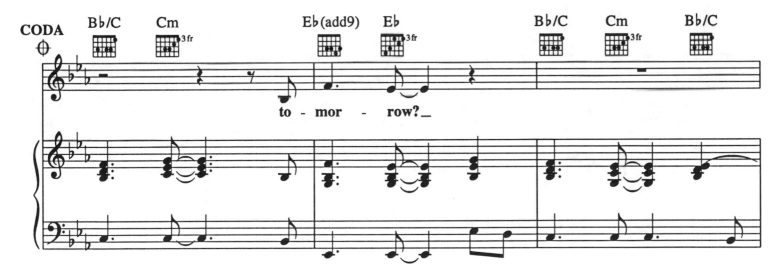

CODA

to - mor - row? _

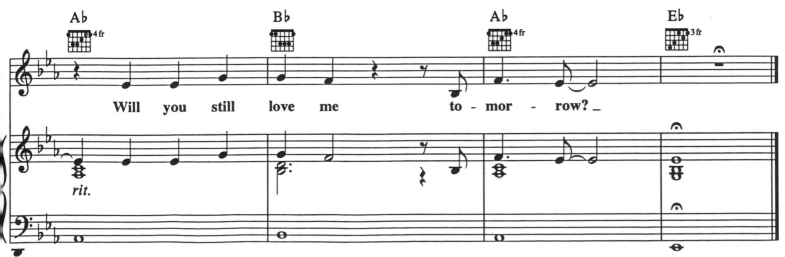

Will you still love me to - mor - row? _

DO WAH DIDDY DIDDY

Words and Music by JEFF BARRY
and ELLIE GREENWICH

1

D7

fine, (Yeah, yeah) She looked good, she looked fine, and I near-ly lost my mind. Be -
door, (Yeah, yeah) We walked on to my door, and she

2

D7   G   Em

3

stayed a lit-tle more.   My, my, my, my,   I knew we were fall-in' in

more broadly

C   D7

3

love,   My, my, my, my,_____   I told her all the things I was

G   C   G

dream-in' of._____   Now we're to-geth-er near-ly ev-'ry sin-gle day, Sing-in'

DON'T MAKE ME OVER

Lyric by HAL DAVID
Music by BURT BACHARACH

Rock Ballad

Don't make me o - ver, _____
Don't make me o - ver, _____
now that I can't make it with -
now that I'd do an - y - thing

out you.
for you.

Don't make me o - ver, _____
Don't make me o - ver, _____

I (WHO HAVE NOTHING)

English language lyric by
JERRY LIEBER and MIKE STOLLER
Original Italian lyric by MOGOL
Music by CARLO DONIDA

Moderately slow, with feeling

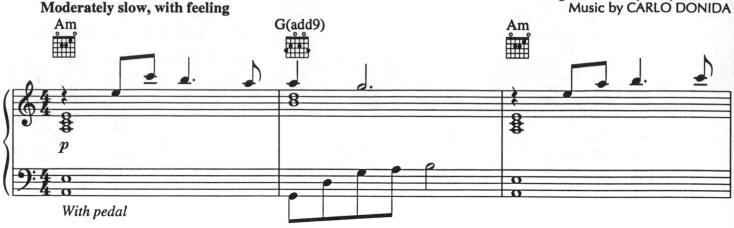

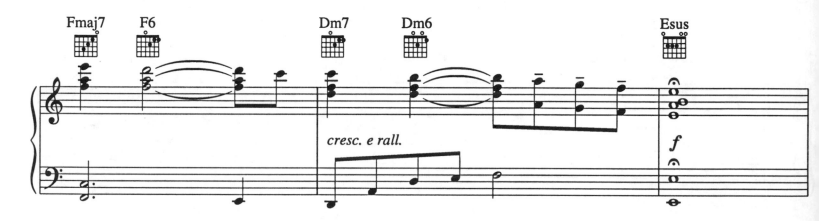

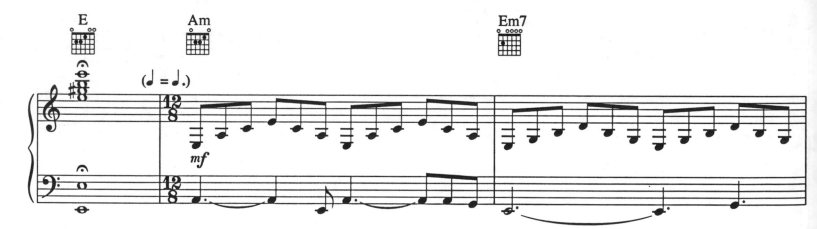

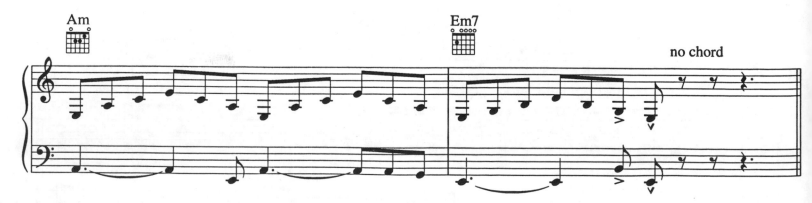

D.S. al Coda

love you. __

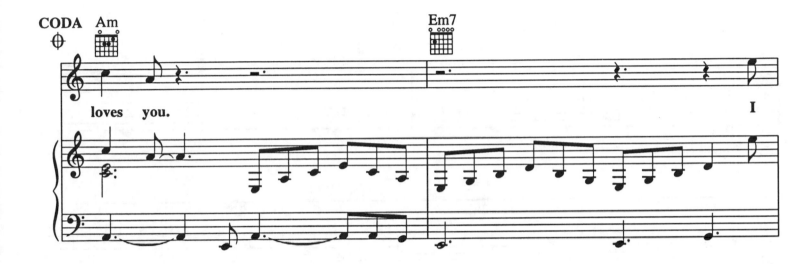

CODA

loves you.

I

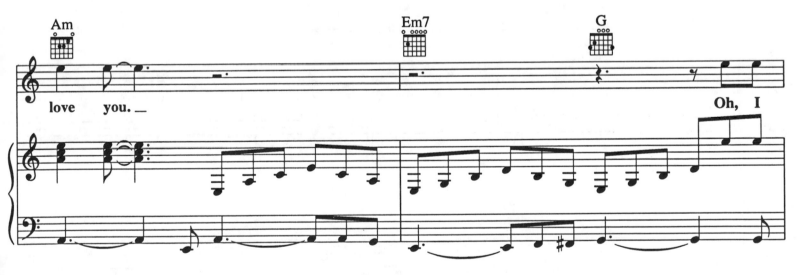

love you. __

Oh, I

love you, __

I who have noth-ing. _____

rit.

DO YOU KNOW THE WAY TO SAN JOSE?

Lyric by HAL DAVID
Music by BURT BACHARACH

Weeks turn in - to years. How quick _ they pass, _____ and all the stars_
Dreams turn in - to dust and blow _ a - way, _____ and there you are_

_ that nev - er were ___ are park - ing cars ___ and pump - ing gas. _
_ with-out a friend. _ You pack your car ___ and ride_ a - way. _

I've got lots of

friends in San _ Jo - se.

Repeat and Fade

RIVER DEEP - MOUNTAIN HIGH

Words and Music by JEFF BARRY,
ELLIE GREENWICH and PHIL SPECTOR

Fast and steady

no chord

When you were a lit-tle girl, ___ you had a rag-
you have a pup-

-doll, the on-ly doll ___ you've ev-er owned.
-py that al-ways fol-lowed you ___ a-round?

Now, I
Well, I

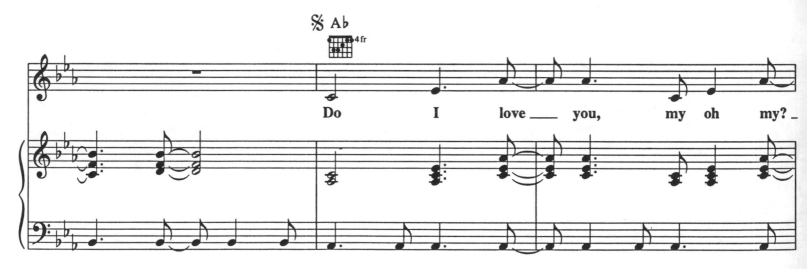

moun - tain high. ___

If I lost ___ you, would I cry? ___

Oh, how I love you, ba - by, _____

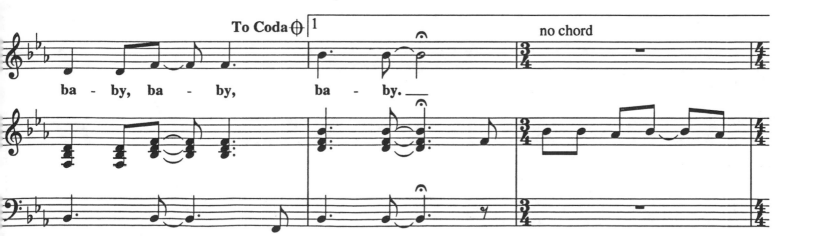

To Coda ⊕ | 1   no chord

ba - by, ba - by, ba - by. ___

- er loves ___ the spring, ___ and I love you, ba -

- by, like ___ the rob - in loves ___ to sing. ___

I love you, ba - by, like ___ a school - boy loves his

pie, and I love you, ba - by, riv - er deep

and moun-tain high.

D.S. al Coda

CODA

ba - by.

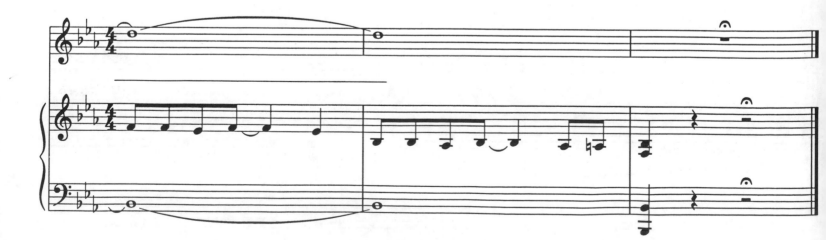

SPANISH HARLEM

Words and Music by JERRY LEIBER
and PHIL SPECTOR

1 thru the con - crete but soft and sweet_ and dream - ing._____

2 her as she grows_____ in my gar - den._____

A GROOVY KIND OF LOVE

Words and Music by TONI WINE
and CAROLE BAYER SAGER

When I'm feel-in' blue, all I have to do is take a look at
want to, you can turn me on to an-y-thing you

you, and then I'm not so blue. When you're close to me, I can feel your
want to, an-y-time at all. When I taste your lips, oh, I start to

heart beat. I can hear you breath-ing in my ear.
shiv-er, can't con-trol the quiv-er-ing in-side. Would-n't you a-

gree, ba-by, you and me,

we got a groov-y kind of love? We got a groov-y kind of

love. An-y-time you love. *Instrumental solo*

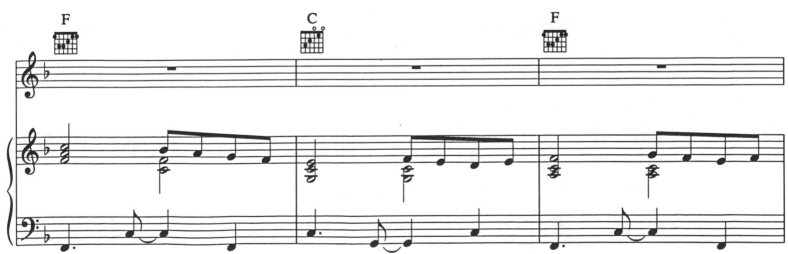

I love __ you. I love __ you.

I love __ you; it's true. __ When I'm feel-in' blue, all I have to

do is take a look at you, and then I'm not so blue. When I'm in your

arms, noth-ing seems to mat-ter. If the world would shat-ter, I don't

care. Would-n't you a - gree, ba - by, you and

me, we got a groov-y kind of love.

We got a groov-y kind of love.

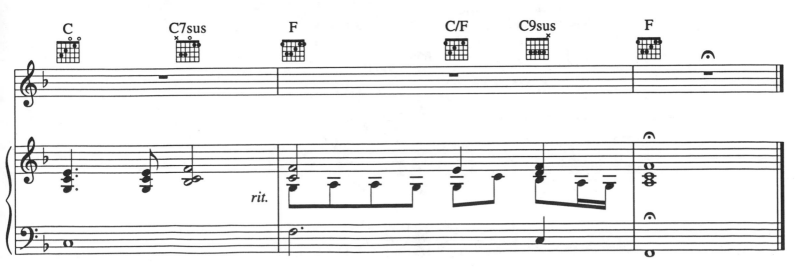

rit.

SWEETS FOR MY SWEET

Words and Music by DOC POMUS
and MORT SHUMAN

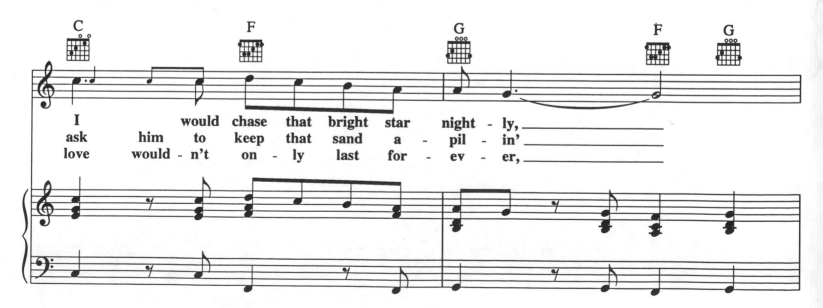

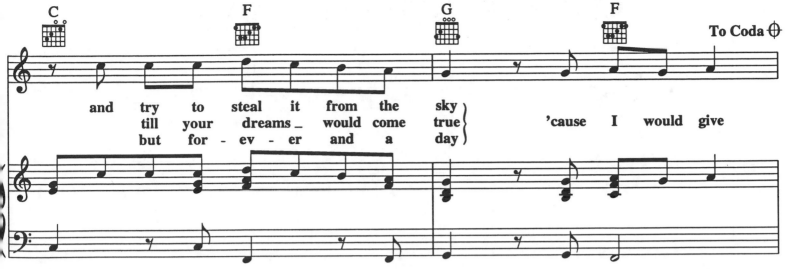

To Coda ⊕

and try to steal it from the sky ⎫
till your dreams ___ would come true ⎬ 'cause I would give
but for - ev - er and a day ⎭

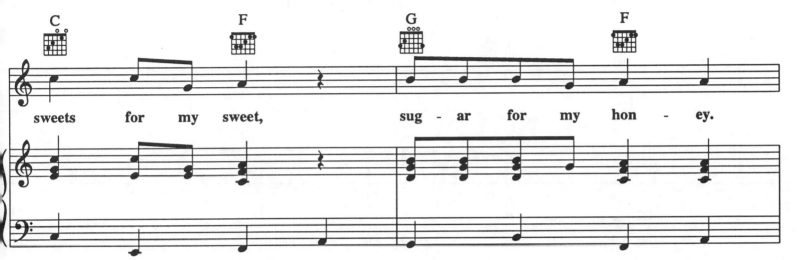

sweets for my sweet, sug - ar for my hon - ey.

Your tast - y kiss thrills me so. ___

Sweets for my sweet, sug - ar for my hon - ey.

I'll nev-er ev-er let you go. ___

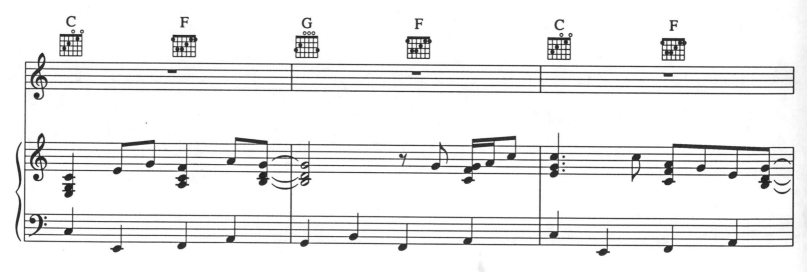

If you

D.S. al Coda

If you

CODA

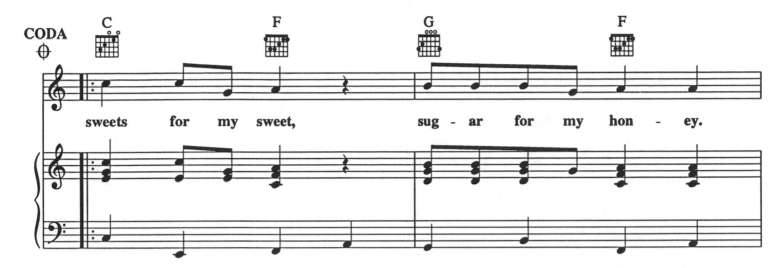

sweets for my sweet, sug - ar for my hon - ey.

Your tast - y kiss thrills me so. _____

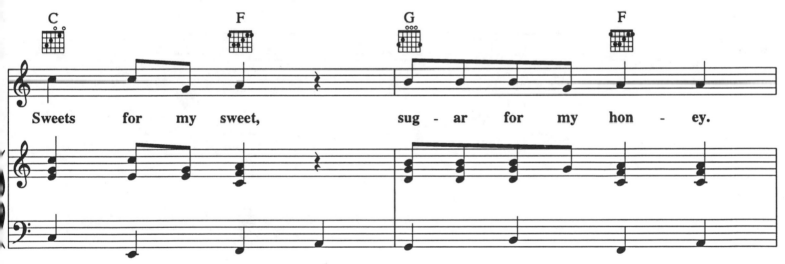

Sweets for my sweet, sug - ar for my hon - ey.

Repeat and Fade

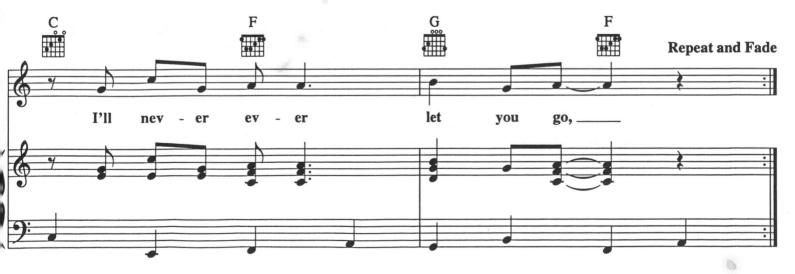

I'll nev - er ev - er let you go, _____

TEN LONELY GUYS

Words and Music by BOB FELDMAN, JERRY GOLDSTEIN,
RICHARD GOTTEHRER, STANLEY KAHAN, EDDIE SNYDER,
LOCKIE EDWARDS, JR., LARRY WEISS, CLIFF ADAMS,
WES FARRELL and NEIL DIAMOND

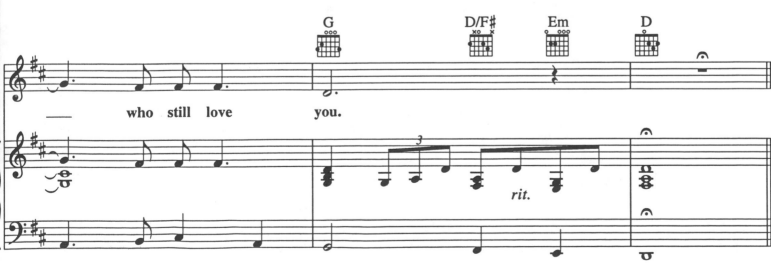

SAVE THE LAST DANCE FOR ME

Words and Music by DOC POMUS
and MORT SHUMAN

much.   You can

dance,   go and car - ry on __ till the night is gone __ till it's

time   to   go. __   If {he/she} asks   if you're

all   a - lone, __   can {he/she} take   you home, __ you've got to

HAPPY BIRTHDAY SWEET SIXTEEN

Words and Music by HOWARD GREENFIELD
and NEIL SEDAKA